How To
MOTIVATE
EVERYONE

Family, Friends, Co-workers, (Even Yourself)

Jay Arthur

Upgrade Your KnowWare!

Published by LifeStar Publishing
2244 S. Olive St.
Denver, CO 80224
(888) 468-1537
lifestar@rmi.net
www.quantum-i.com

ISBN 1-884180-17-5

Publisher's Cataloging-in-Publication Data
Arthur, Jay
    How to Motivate Everyone: Friends, Family, Co-Workers,
    Even Yourself! / by Jay Arthur
        p.   cm.
    Includes bibliographical references.
    ISBN 1-884180-17-5
    1. Employee motivation   I. Title
    2. Organizational change
    3. Influence <Psychology>
    4. Persuasion <Psychology>
    5. Interpersonal relations
HF5549.5M63A47   2001
658.3'14–DC20   00-193560 CIP

Printed in the United States of America
10 9 8 7 6 5 4 3 2 1

Contents

Preface   7

1. Five Levels of Motivation   9

2. Values and Power Words   29

3. Achiever–Problem Solver   39

4. Leader–Follower   53

5. Innovator–Processor   63

6. Doer–Thinker   69

7. Evolutionary–Revolutionary   77

8. Dreamer–Realist–Critic   97

9. The Power of Beliefs   105

10. Creating Desire   129

Appendix A–Questions, Answers, Motivation   137

About The Author

 Jay Arthur, the KnowWare® Man, works with people that want to master the mysteries of the mind, and companies that want jungle medicine for the corporate soul. Jay is a certified master and health practitioner of Neuro-Linguistic Programming (NLP) and an Inkan shaman.

Growing up in Tucson, Arizona, Jay was obsessed with *how* people do things well. As a student of human nature, Jay began to study what works and what doesn't. He began to look for clues to human excellence. Jay would be almost 40 before he began to find the answers he was looking for. He graduated with a degree in systems engineering and spent the next 20 years developing software for the phone company. Becoming increasingly dissatisfied with the results he was creating in the world, Jay began again to look for solutions to his discomfort. He had spent the last 20 years looking outside himself for answers, so he began in earnest to look within. What he found and still finds continues to astound him.

Jay found that the brain is *like a computer* and the mind is *like software*, but the software of the mind, what Jay calls KnowWare, is much more rich and sophisticated than COBOL, HTML, or JAVA. While computers are binary (two bits: 0,1), human DNA is quadrinary (four bits: A, T, C, G). Your mind uses seeing, hearing, feeling, smelling, and tasting as part of its programming "code." The mind, just like software, has modular routines that handle everything from tying a shoelace to driving a car while your talking on your cell phone and planning your next meeting. Some of this KnowWare is elegant and very useful; some of it is defective and causes problems; and some of it is missing.

Jay found that if you change your mind, you can change your life. It's possible to shed the past, design your destiny, and succeed at anything if you take the time to learn to do it well.

One of the keys to success is motivation and this book distills the best of what Jay has discovered about how to motivate everyone.

"Very good, Sedgewick. Now let's see you bark and roll over."

Preface

Have you ever been talking with someone and you know they're speaking English, but you just can't understand them? Does it seem like they're speaking a foreign language? Or, do you understand part of what they are saying, but not all of it? How much rapport do you feel with this person? How much time do you want to spend with them? Do you trust their ideas?

As you will discover, they aren't from another country or planet, they just run their mind differently than you do and it *shows* in their language. Stephen Covey said: "Seek first to understand, then to be understood." So you might consider that understanding other people will give you improved tools to motivate anyone in new and better ways, without spending a dime.

In *Motivate Everyone* you'll discover the five levels of human motivation: capabilities, beliefs, values, identity, and mission. Each one is increasingly important for creating motivation without manipulation. You can't motivate someone if your suggestion or direction conflicts with the person's internal maps of reality. Once you understand a person's beliefs, values, and capabilities, you can align your idea, product, or service with their reality to make it easy to for them to be motivated.

Each person has a vast array of values which vary from situation to situation. You can discover someone's values using simple questions like: "What's important to you about your home or work?" In chapter two you'll learn how to discover and use people's values to motivate them to take action.

At the level of capabilities, there are five mental, motivation programs that you can detect with simple questions like "How do you know you've done a good job?" In chapters three through seven you'll learn how to use the answers to these questions to trigger motivation with simple, but irresistible phrases.

High performance teams consist of three personality styles: dreamers, realists, and critics. Each has a unique set of values and motivation triggers. In chapter eight you'll learn how to reduce conflict and increase team productivity using the skills you've learned.

Chapter nine introduces the limiting beliefs that can inhibit a person's motivation. People sometimes feel hopeless, helpless, worthless, useless, or blameless. Employees sometimes fail to get things done because they believe it's not possible or desirable to do so. They may think they don't know how to do it. They may not think it's their job. Until these limiting beliefs are changed, motivation is next to impossible. In this chapter you'll learn how to use simple questions and powerful language to discover and transform limiting beliefs with ease.

Sometimes people fail to get motivated because they aren't sure what they want. In chapter 10 we'll explore ways to create desire and passion that will propel a person into action.

Thousands of people have learned these skills, so decide for yourself which ones will help you break through to new and improved levels of performance. Haven't you waited long enough to learn how to motivate everyone more effectively?

Chapter 1

Five Levels of Motivation

Motivation not Manipulation

Invariably, the first question out of someone's mouth is: "Isn't this manipulative?" The answer is: "It can be, depending on *your* intention." First, consider that everyone is trying to influence and motivate everyone else all the time. Parents influence kids to go to bed or college, or to do a host of things that kids may not care to do. Teachers motivate children to learn. Advertising motivates people to buy products and services. Managers motivate employ-

WIIFM vs WBCG

ees. Employees try to influence the boss. Laws encourage and discourage various behaviors. Influence and motivation exists in almost every situation. Whether these skills are used to manipulate or motivate is a matter of personal *intention*.

What makes these skills *manipulative*?
Answer: WIIFM–What's in it for me, self-serving, self-interest.

What makes these behaviors *motivational*?
Answer: WBCG–What's best for the common good? You, me and all concerned?

Do you make the kids go to bed so that you can get some peace and quiet (WIIFM)? Or so that they will be rested and ready for school the next day (WBCG)? Do you motivate employees so that you can get a promotion (WIIFM)? Or do you motivate employees so that the company will perform better and everyone will benefit from the increased market share and profits (WBCG)? Do you try to sell products so that you can make more money (WIIFM)? Or do you sell products to meet the needs, wants, and desires of your customers and community (WBCG)?

The choice is up to you. One of life's paradoxes is that you can only get to WIIFM by focusing your efforts on WBCG. As the motivational speakers say: "You can get whatever you want, if you help enough other people get what they want."

Motivation can be a seemingly complex issue, but using existing research, you'll find that it can be broken

Five Levels of Motivation

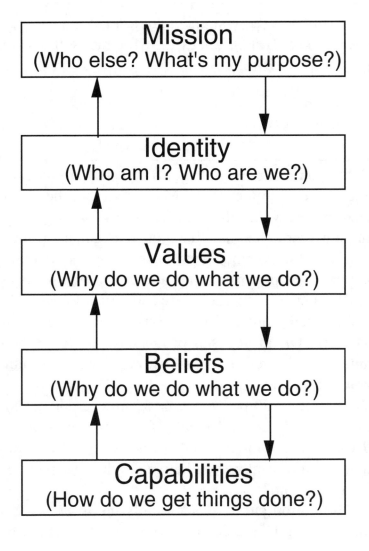

Mission
(Who else? What's my purpose?)

Identity
(Who am I? Who are we?)

Values
(Why do we do what we do?)

Beliefs
(Why do we do what we do?)

Capabilities
(How do we get things done?)

down into five levels of the human mind–capabilities, values, beliefs, identity, and mission.

Mission

Everyone has a life purpose–what the shamans call your "original medicine." This is the work of the soul. People often sacrifice their purpose for a job that pays money, but they become disenchanted as they move farther away from their purpose. It's difficult to motivate anyone if the action conflicts with their life purpose. The secret is to understand and align with that mission and purpose.

Identity

Every person has a sense of identity, of who they are. Charles Faulkner found that people have an internal 3-D experience of who they are and the mythic forces that shape their life. If you try to motivate someone to do something that conflicts with their identity, you are in for a struggle. A VW bug person will not buy a Corvette or a Jaguar, because it's not aligned with their identity. Again the issue is to find ways to align your outcome with the person's identity.

The secret to using identity to motivate yourself and other people is to get a commitment. We all have an obsessive desire to appear consistent with what we've already done; to justify our prior behavior. Once you make a written commitment to do, achieve, accomplish, behave or whatever, you tend to live up to the commitment. This is what Robert Cialdini calls "commitment consistency" (1993). We tend to behave in alignment with who we think

Motives

Everyone has talent. What is rare is the courage to follow the talent to the dark place where it leads.
-Erica Jong

we are. The more public the commitment, the more lasting the effects.

Why does goal setting work? Because you write down the goal and a due date, which is your commitment. Then you will tend to behave in ways to achieve those goals and outcomes. Failure to set a goal or a due date makes it easy to procrastinate, delay, or put off doing the things you need to do. People often find that the act of writing goals leads to their fulfillment. They return a year later and find their goals are complete.

So consider writing a commitment to be, do, achieve, have, get, learn, or relate with the level of quality that you want in your life. Just write it down and you will tend to live up to your own expectations.

So will other people. If you get a written agreement or commitment, people will tend to live up to it. Why do magazine contests get us engaged in cutting things out and moving them onto the order form? Commitment! Why do sales people want us to test drive a car? Commitment! Just be aware that small, seemingly inconsequential acts of commitment and seemingly harmless concessions lead to subtle shifts in identity and behavior.

Values

If you try to motivate someone to do something that violates one of their values, especially a core value, it simply won't work unless you find a way to align the action with their values.

Values also influence our choices. We are more likely to believe someone who is attractive or an authority. We tend to like people who are attractive, because we want to be like them. We tend to convey more authority on people

Motivate Everyone

*You can motivate
anyone to do anything
if it matches their
internal mental
programming!*

with initials like M.D. or Ph.D. behind their name. Nurses rarely question doctors. Copilots rarely question pilots. We tend to believe actors in television commercials who dress like doctors. These are two value patterns Cialdini calls "liking" and "authority."

We also tend to value things that are scarce, rare, or limited in availability. If it's hard to get, it *must* be better. Think antiques, rare coins, or that hard-to-find Christmas toy for the kids. Anything that becomes less available becomes more attractive. This is a pattern Cialdini calls "scarcity."

How can you make your product or service seem scarce or rare, hard to get? To ignite a feeding frenzy, chum the waters. The U.S. Mint, for example, let out a few of the new dollar coins imprinted with the Sacajawea on the front and a quarter on the back. The value of this error to a coin collector was tens of thousands of dollars. The value to the mint: priceless! In the chapter on values, we'll explore how to ask a simple question to discover people's values and how to use them ecologically and ethically to motivate.

Beliefs

If you try to motivate someone to do something that conflicts with their beliefs, especially their limiting beliefs, it won't work either. There are five limiting beliefs:

- Hopeless   It's not possible.
- Helpless   I can't do it.
- Worthless   I don't deserve it.
- Useless   I don't want or desire it.
- Blameless   I'm not responsible for getting or doing it.

What Moves You?

*All that we do is
done with an eye to
something else.*
-Aristotle

Most beliefs help us, but limiting beliefs stop us from achieving our dreams and ambitions. All beliefs are formed, over time, through our interaction with people and our surroundings.

Here's the good news:

Beliefs can be changed!

In the chapter on beliefs, we'll explore how to determine the structure of a limiting belief and then transform it into a neutral or useful belief using "sleight of mouth."

One of the most common beliefs is the belief in fair play. Cialdini calls this *reciprocity*. If someone does something for us, we feel indebted to them. Even a small favor can be traded for a larger return favor later on. Sales people use "free" samples of a product to induce us to buy the product. Even test driving a car is a free sample.

Another way that sales people use the fair play rule is by making concessions. They show you the most expensive product first, then when you reject it, they retreat to a less expensive product which you will be more likely to buy, because they have already made a concession, so it's your turn to make one to them.

Capabilities

Getting people motivated at the level of capabilities is relatively easy. It involves understanding the five key motivational styles. Five chapters of this book are dedicated to understanding and using each of these styles.

At the level of capabilities, beware of the "herd instinct." This is what Cialdini calls "social proof." Each of us tends to act in alignment with what other people

Leadership

*A great leader is a man
who has the ability to
get other people to do
what they don't want to
do and like it.*
-Harry Truman

think is acceptable or correct. The more people who support an idea or action, the more it will influence everyone. Kids in school like to wear the same clothes. Each generation will drive similar cars, wear similar clothes, live in similar housing or communities.

Cialdini also provides data to show that even extreme issues, suicides that make the front page, will cause an increase in suicides over the next 10 days. As much as we value individuality, we are also shaped by the herd instinct, and we can motivate others to align with the herd. In the chapters on capabilities, we will explore the five motivation programs: *toward-away, internal-external, options-procedures, passive-active, response to change*, and even more about everyone's hot buttons—*values*.

There are a few key mental programs that run in the background of your mind. These "motivation programs" filter your experiences and trigger your responses. Depending on how an idea is presented, your mind will quickly decide to ignore, pay attention to, or act on the idea. If a new career opportunity arises, for example, do you focus on the potential benefits or problems associated with the change? Do you ask other people what you should do or do you check inside and decide for yourself? Do you go after career opportunities or do you let them find you? Are you following a linear career path or do you consider lots of options? Do you want the same kind of work, a better position, or something new?

In any relationship, these motivation programs can cause conflict. One spouse may want to take a promising new job with a higher salary and more influential title; the other spouse may worry about how it will affect their

Hope and Fear

Men can be stimulated by hope and driven by fear, but the hope and the fear must be vivid and immediate if they are to be effective without producing weariness.
-Bertrand Russell

Motivation Triggers

1. Toward-Away - goal achievers or problem solvers.

2. Internal-External - decisive leadership or compliant followership.

3. Options-Procedures - choices or process

4. Active-Passive - self-starting or other-initiating.

5. Sameness-Progress-Difference - same, improved, or new.

relationship, the kids, etc. In a business partnership, one partner wants to go after promising opportunities and the other partner brings up all of the possible problems associated with pursing that client or market. Either side may believe that the other party isn't listening to them or respecting their opinion. These mental motivations are neither "bad" nor "good." Each is useful in the appropriate situation.

Each motivation program determines how you jump into action. Do you get moving by imagining the benefits of what you're going to do or do you imagine the consequences of not doing it?

Each motivation program also expresses itself through unique language. To develop rapport, we need to use the language that matches our audience: "This house is *close* to schools, shopping, and parks." Compare this with: "This house *isn't too far* from schools, shopping, or parks." One is *toward* language; the other, *away from.*

Toward people move *toward* pleasure and possibility. They are the visionaries, the achievers. They often put the past behind them and constantly move toward their goals and objectives. Toward people can get into trouble by not sufficiently evaluating ideas before implementing them. They can learn to look before they leap or work with an "away-from" to critique their plans.

Away from people move *away from* possible pain. They make good problem solvers, editors, and evaluators. Moving away is like driving a car by looking in the rear view mirror. Away from people often miss oppor-

How Do You Decide?

Nothing is more difficult, and therefore more precious, than to be able to decide.
-Napolean I

tunities by overanalyzing the possible problems associated with them. They can learn to set goals and review them periodically to stay focused on achieving them.

While many a good idea has been killed by criticism, ideas and plans first need to be created. Then, when as fully formed as possible, they can be subjected to scrutiny and criticism. Without this evaluation, they might remain ill-formed and fail.

Internal people are often strong leaders who make decisions easily based on their own internal values. They gather information and use their intuition to make decisions. They can get into trouble by not gathering enough information from other sources before making a decision. Internals can benefit from asking people they trust for information. In this way, they can learn how to make collaborative decisions.

External people rely on others to help them decide what to do. They tend to focus on and value what other people think. At the extreme, they can be easily influenced to buy things they don't want, or to do things that they don't agree with. They may be overly concerned with what others will think of their actions and choices. They can learn how to establish their own criteria for decisions.

Procedures people like to follow a step-by-step process and obey the rules. All businesses make money through a combination of innovation and following procedures. Pro-

What About Change?

*The world owes
all its onward
impulses to men ill
at ease.*

*The happy man
inevitably confines
himself within
ancient limits.*
-Nathaniel Hawthorne

cedural people get into trouble when their existing process stops working. They can learn how to ask for help and better ways of working.

Options people are innovators. They *have to* try new ways of doing things. Their motto is: "There has to be a better way." Options people get into trouble when they try to reinvent successful processes.

Active people like to jump into the fray. They like to be doing some thing, getting things done. They often seem highly moti-

vated. They can become highly paid "fire fighters," reacting swiftly to problems. Active people can get into trouble by not giving as much thought to important issues as they give to critical ones. They can learn to prioritize their efforts.

Passive people wait for the dust to settle before they engage. These people get into trouble by putting things off until the timing seems right. By doing so, they may not accomplish the goals they have always desired. They keep waiting for something external to get them started.

Sameness people want the world to stay the same. They resist change because their tolerance for change is low. They can stay in the same job, work function, marriage or whatever for long periods of time. They tolerate major changes every 10 years and initiate them every 15-25 and represent only 5% of the population. Their password is "same." These people are "settlers."

Progress people like continuous improvement or gradual change. They represent 65% of the population. They tolerate annual changes but they resist radical changes. They tend to initiate changes every 5-7 years. Their watchwords are "better," "improved," or "progress." They discover improvements and integrate them into their work and life. These people are the "paradigm pioneers."

Difference people are innovators, entrepreneurs, and revolutionaries. They like to initiate change every 18-24 months and make up the remaining 30% of the population. They resist stability. They initiate change every one-two years. They can learn to be satisfied with smaller changes--remodeling a room rather than buying a new house. Their watchwords are "new" or "different." They are the "paradigm shifters."

These five motivation programs–toward-away, internal-external, options-procedures, active-passive, and sameness-progress-difference–have tremendous power once you understand the simple words and phrases that can trigger each of these motivations. Each person you meet will have a unique combination of these programs for different situations. As you'll discover in the next several chapters, it's easy and fun to ask simple questions to discover these programs. Then you'll learn how easy it is to use simple words and phrases to trigger motivation in everyone.

Chapter 2

Values and Power Words

One of our most powerful motivation programs revolves around core values. Do you like to spend your time relating to people, being in a place, doing activities, learning knowledge, or getting, collecting or having things? What you value will determine how and where you spend your time. Values are what get you up in the morning and keep you going.

Power Words

Ask yourself the following questions:
• What's important about a job, career, or work?
• What's important about a marriage or friendship?

What's A Value?

Nothing is intrinsically valuable; the value of everything is attributed to it, assigned to it from outside...by people.
-John Barth

- What's important about where you live?
- What's important about the kind of car you drive?
- What's important about what you know or learn?

The exact words or phrases you use to answer these questions are the words you've mentally *attached* to your values. In the jargon of the Internet, they are hotlinked to your core values. These power words and phrases will get you motivated. Once someone knows your power words, all they have to do is use *your* power words to describe their product, service, job, or relationship, and you will find their offering much more desirable. In many ways you will feel *compelled* to get involved with their offering because it's part of who you are and what you want at the deepest level.

The question you can ask to discover anyone's values around a particular topic is:

What's important about *topic*?

Here *topic* can be job, marriage, relationships, friends, dogs, cats, music, cities, travel, sports, knowledge, learning, house, cars, jewelry, etc. Values can change dramatically from one context to the next.

The *exact words or phrases* a person uses to respond to your question tell you the words they associate with their values. In grade school we were taught *not* to use the same words, but rather to paraphrase the other person's words. If you want to motivate the other person, paraphrasing is a mistake; a similar word simply will not mean the same thing, it will not be "hot linked" to the same internal *values* as their word or phrase. So, if you want to motivate someone, use their power words, not your own.

Questions & Answers

*Everything is worth
what its purchaser
will pay for it.*
-Publilius Syrus

Ask: What's important to you ...?

Listen: Power Words and Phrases

Connect: Your project or issue with
their power words or phrases

In some marketing circles, this is known as "cracking the code," because the ideal word or phrase to maximize response to an ad is often hard to discover. You're like a cryptographer decoding secret transmissions. In direct mail, one headline can pull twenty times more orders than another. Why? Because one cracks the code and one doesn't. Marketing guru Jay Abraham says that "we have no right to determine what the customer wants or is willing to pay for." We have to ask and test!

If you ask someone "what's important about your job?" they may reply:

- *challenge* and *opportunity*
- *safety* and *security*
- *working with people*
- *live where I want to live*
- *do what I want to do*
- *learn new skills* and *grow my abilities*
- *have the kind of house and life-style I want*

In each case, the words or phrases are directly linked to their core values around work. These words and phrases can then be used to motivate their involvement in work priorities:

- This project will be both *challenging* and a great *opportunity* for team members.
- This project will create the kind of *safety* and *security* the company needs for ongoing success.
- This project will involve *working with people*: clients, customers, suppliers, and leadership.

Notice how it's possible to use the other person's exact phrase in a sentence to connect their core values

Life Values

"Gentlemen, this is a power restaurant. If you must discuss your families, please keep your voices down."

with the new project. Once you do so, they are more inclined to want to do it because it matches their internal values (WIIFM), and you've motivated them to do what's best for the common good! Think back to your answers to the questions on the first page of this chapter. Which ones would get you inspired to take on this or any project?

It Depends...

Occasionally, in response to the question "What's important about your job?" a person will answer: "It depends." When this happens, they've just told you that the context or situation you asked about isn't specific enough. So, ask: "What are the situations on your job where it's different?" They may respond: "When I'm with a customer it's important to help them solve problems, but when I'm with an employee it's important to coach them to solve their own problems." *It depends* will always tell you to dig deeper and get more specific.

Core Values

The five most common answers to the "What's important about..." question fall into the broad categories of people, places, activities, knowledge, and things.

"**People**" people are most interested in their relationships. They prize friendship, family, and connection above everything else. They tend to get interested in going, getting, doing, being, learning, or having because of the people they know. They may find it hard to leave unsatisfactory relationships and jobs be-

Values Move You

What's important to you...?

1. People or relating

2. Places or being

3. Activities or doing

4. Knowledge or learning

5. Things or getting/having

cause of their respect for the people involved. Taken to extremes, they can become co-dependent and spend their lives solely in the service of others. They may do things contrary to their own good.

"**Places**" people are most concerned about where they live–near the mountains, the ocean, and so on–or just being. They have a strong sense of being grounded. At the extreme, these people will not relocate, even when staying will mean a drop in their standard of living and moving means an improvement in their life style.

"**Activity**" people are most interested in doing things. They plan their time around sports, exercise, hobbies, and other activities. They may belong to health clubs, engage in team or individual sports, or just work around the house. They like being in motion. At the extreme, they may overexert or overcommit themselves.

"**Knowledge**" people are most interested in what they can learn and know about the people, places, activities, and things in their lives. They tend to enjoy bookstores and libraries. They attend courses frequently. At the extreme, these people become professional students and never apply the knowledge they have learned.

"**Things**" people are most interested in what they get, have, own or collect-- art, cars, homes, clothes, and so on. They love to shop. They like catalogs. They watch cable TV sales programs. They are driven to make money to acquire things. Taken to extremes, these people become shop-aholics. They will charge their credit cards up to the limit and keep them there.

Most values can be categorized in one of these five core values: people, places, activities, knowledge, or things.

Values Question

Remember, the question to find out someone's values and the power words coupled to them is simple: "What's important about...?" Just fill in the blank with the area of life you'd like to understand more completely. Then write down the answer *exactly as you hear it*. You can also do this with your own life to find out what you value.

Motivation

To motivate people using their values, all you have to do is use the power words or phrases they supply. Simply find a way to align your product, service, outcome, or mission to their values and it becomes much easier for them to get motivated to work on it with you. In the process, you'll also build better relationships, achieve more, learn more, and become more successful in all aspects of your life.

Chapter 3

Achiever - Problem Solver

Some years ago, I boarded a flight from Boston to Denver. I had an aisle seat in the middle of a DC-10. To my right sat a six-year-old girl with long, curly blonde hair. Her mother, a brunette sat to her right. All was quiet until the plane took off.

Then, the little girl started kicking the seat in front of her, gently at first and then with more vigor. I saw the businessman look back and scowl. The girl's mother told her to *stop* kicking the man's chair. With renewed vigor, the girl started kicking faster and harder.

Having just learned some of the techniques you'll discover in this chapter, I decided to try them out. I turned

Achiever-
Problem Solver

*The best stimulus for
running ahead is to
have something we
must run from.*
-Eric Hoffer

Achiever–Problem Solver

Achievers are easily motivated to set and achieve goals. Goal setting is ideal for them.

Problem Solvers get motivated to overcome difficulties and avoid obstacles. Goals help them stay focused, but will not trigger them into action. Acquiring wealth, for a problem solver, is not as exciting as avoiding poverty in retirement.

to the girl and said: "*Don't stop* kicking that man's chair"...and her little leg swung to a stop. She knew she'd been had, but she didn't know how, so she started kicking again.

I said: "*Don't* stop kicking that man's chair"...and her leg swung to a stop again. She frowned briefly and then she smiled.

"What's your name?" she asked.

"It's Jay," I said.

"No it's not," she said, her smile growing wider.

I said, "You're right, it's not."

"Yes it is," she said, the beginning of a frown creasing her brow.

"No it's not," I replied.

"Yes it is!" she demanded. "You're name's Jay! Say it."

"Whatever you say," I replied.

By this time, her mother was looking at me with that how-do-you-know-how-to-run-my-child look. The little girl was fine the rest of the flight. Someone had finally understood her.

This is an extreme example called mismatching, but offers many clues into the language pattern of the problem solver. While most books on motivation try to get you to move toward possibilities and opportunities, they miss the 40% of the population that get motivated by avoiding the consequences of action or inaction.

Motivation

Do you move *toward* pleasure or *away from* pain? Pleasure, unfortunately, is often only the promise of a

Questions & Answers

Question: What's important about ...?
Listen: power words and phrases

Question: Why is that *power word* important?
Listen: get, have, achieve (toward) avoid, prevent, wouldn't, can't (away)

Motivating Language

Achiever	Problem Solver
achieve	avoid
accomplish	prevent
get	not

future reward. Pain is much more immediate. Toward people see the glass as half full while the away-froms see the glass as half empty. Which one are you?

Achievers move *toward* opportunity and possibility. They often create the next step in human evolution, processes, or technology. They can, however, jump too easily into relationships, partnerships, or new ventures without clearly understanding the consequences of their actions.

Problem solvers move away from possible pain. They tend to be better at analyzing and solving problems. They can also create new things by amplifying the consequences of *not doing it*. They can be motivated to avoid ending up in the same circumstances as their parents or friends. I know some very successful people who get motivated this way! To achieve goals, problem solvers need to periodically refocus on their objectives, not just the consequences.

There is an old story of putting a frog in a pan of tepid water. If you raise the temperature slowly enough, you can literally boil the frog. Away-froms have this problem. If the *change* in pain isn't different enough, they won't jump into action to change things. Consider cult leaders or abusive partners who start with small indiscretions and increase them slowly to the boiling point.

It might seem logical that *toward* would be more associated with the future and that *away from* might be more associated with the past, but people can be motivated toward doing the same thing over and over again

Mistakes

Flops are part of life's menu and I've never been a girl to miss out on any of the courses.
-Rosalind Russell

because they were successful in the past. Similarly, people can be motivated away from the future consequences of doing something.

To influence **achievers**, use language that talks about the benefits (pleasure) of achieving an outcome. To influence **problem solvers**, talk about how to avoid the consequences of not achieving the outcome.

Tag Questions

Another way to use both *toward* and *away from* language in a sentence is by using a tag question: "Sounds like a good idea, doesn't it? You agree, don't you? That would be a good choice, wouldn't it?" In each case the toward is followed by an away-from tag question.

Family and Friends

On Friday night, my wife and I usually have a conversation about what to do:

"Well," I say, "we could *go* to a movie or we could *go* out to eat"

She says: "I *wouldn't* want to see anything *too violent* or *eat too much.*"

As you'll learn, my wife and I are about as different as they come when it comes to language patterns. There are two opposing motivation programs concealed in this short dialog. When it comes to Friday night:

Jay	Shirley
Achiever	Problem Solver

My language is *outcome-oriented*: go, see, eat. Her language is *away-from*: avoiding the discomfort of violent movies or eating too much.

Risk Management

"'Don't worry'! All you can tell me is 'Don't Worry'?"

To motivate my wife, all I have to do is figure out what we could avoid by doing what I suggest. I need to use a lot of "not" words: don't, couldn't, wouldn't, etc.

"We *wouldn't* want to buy a car that costs *too* much."

"We *wouldn't* want our daughter to get a bad education, but we *wouldn't* want to spend a fortune on an out-of-state school. We wouldn't want her to be *too* far away."

Notice how these two sentences illuminate the possible downsides of a new car or an out-of-state school. Problem solvers can take this kind of language and find optimal solutions. (Both daughters went to instate schools less than 90 miles away.)

To motivate me, Shirley has figured out that all she needs to do is keep talking about the goal:

"*Won't* the kitchen *look nice after it's remodeled*?"

The goal: remodel the kitchen. By using the word, *after*, she's also implying that it will be remodeled, it's only a matter of time. By using the word, *won't*, she also handles the possibility of being mismatched (like the girl on the airline).

I have discovered that no matter how quickly these outcomes are achieved, she has an endless list, so I have to manage them to no more than one a year.

Understanding Criticism

We tend to dislike criticism because we often perceive it as blame, but most critics only want to avoid the consequences of behaviors. Their intent is positive, but their approach focuses on the negative. They state issues as general judgements about what is *not* wanted: "We wouldn't want the same sort of problem we had last year."

Team Creativity

Business Applications

Perhaps the most frequent application of toward-away rears its ugly head in meetings. Based on Robert Dilt's study of Walt Disney's creativity strategy, there are three main characters in any effective team:

- **Dreamers** who invent the future
- **Realists** who bring the dream into reality
- **Critics** who help avoid all of the associated problems assoicated with the dream or the plan.

Teams invariably become combative and nonproductive when the critic, the devil's advocate, makes statements about potential problems rather than asking questions about how to avoid the problems. The dialogue goes like this:

Critic: "We *wouldn't* want the same sort of problems we had last year with product X." (The Dreamer and Realist both roll their eyes, because *of course* we wouldn't want that.)

The Critic's statement is actually a thinly veiled "how" question: "How can we avoid the sort of problems we had last year with product X?" Given this sort of question, the Dreamer and Realist can easily figure out how to adjust the dream and the plan to make the product more robust and reliable. Whenever I facilitate a team, I invariably have to serve as an interpreter between the Critic and the other two. Once I understand the Critic's issue, I turn to the rest of the team and say: "So, you're asking *how* can we avoid this kind of problem?" And the rest of the team will nod because they finally understand the issue.

Team Creativity

The ability to convert ideas to things is the secret of outward success.
-Henry Ward Beecher

For critics to become more effective and likable, they need to learn how to turn criticisms into questions: "How can we avoid the kind of problems the neighbors had?" Better yet, explore the positive intent of the criticism (let's say a sturdy house, instead of termites) and ask: "How can we keep the house strong and impervious to termites?"

If you're a Critic, learn to ask "how" questions: "How can we avoid, eliminate, reduce, or prevent this kind of problem?" The Dreamers and Realists will understand your intention more easily and be able to make the needed changes quickly.

If you're a Dreamer or Realist, become an interpreter. Turn the Critic's statement into a question and check: "So, are you asking *how* we can avoid, eliminate, reduce, or prevent this kind of problem?" Once the Critic nods in agreement, explain how you will adapt the dream or plan to incorporate the Critic's concerns.

Another common conflict lies between management (toward) and Union (away from).

Management: "This will open up new market opportunities."

Union: "Our members won't lose their jobs, will they?"

You might consider learning to speak each other's native tongue: "How will expanding into this market create more and better paying jobs for everyone? How will not expanding into this market cost jobs and profits? How will not restricting the size of our business prevent loss of jobs and simultaneously increase profits and revenue?"

Marketing Research

To research customer patterns, you will want to narrow the situation or context. Ask: What's important to you when you decide to:

- hire a consultant?
- buy a similar product or service?
- take a vacation?

Then ask: "Why is that important?" to gather toward-away information. Do you take a vacation to *explore* other cultures or to *get away* from it all? Is it a *journey* or an *escape*?

Conclusions

Possibly the greatest drain on creativity and productivity that I find when working with teams is a conflict between the achievers and the problem solvers (critics and devil's advocates). Both are necessary to a successful marriage, partnership, or team. Without achievers there is no direction. Without problem solvers, there are too many mistakes and failures. Consider where and when you'll next be able to use these language patterns to integrate and align these two seemingly opposing forces into one unstoppable, high performance team. Try not to think about the pain you'll avoid and the success you'll enjoy.

Chapter 4

Leader-Follower

This motivation style determines how you make decisions. Do you ask other people and do what they suggest? Or do you make the decision based on information you've gathered and your own internal wisdom? This style also affects how you know if you're doing well. Do you ask others how you're doing or do you just check inside and know?

Ask yourself: "How do I know I've done a good job?" Is the answer:
- "I just know" (internal) or
- "Other people tell me" (external)?

Leader–Follower

Decide, v. i. To succumb to the preponderance of one set of influences over another set.
  -Ambrose Bierce

Internal–External

Internals need to gather information from people, literature, and instinct on which to base their decision. If you have trouble making a decision, get better information!

Externals ask other people what they should do. They are too easily influenced by salespeople. If you have trouble making a decision, find a trusted advisor (person, internet, or literature, like *Consumer Reports*).

"I just know" is the answer a leader (i.e., internal decision maker) would say. Follower (i.e., external decision maker) usually says something similar to "other people tell me."

Imagine a customer service job–someone answering the phone and taking orders. Would you want that person to be internal or external? If they are overly internal, they may treat the customer rudely. If they are overly external, they may give away the store. A balance would help them first align with the customer (external) and then guide them to useful choices (internal).

Imagine a marriage where one person is internal and the other external. Whose needs get met? Which one is most likely to snap at some point and demand a divorce? Now imagine a relationship where both people are external; they can never make a decision. They just keep asking each other: "What do you want to do?"

When our daughter was a teen, my wife would often have to nag Kelly for days, trying to get her to clean up her room. Teens are trying to develop their own identity, and you want them to become an individual so that you won't have to support them for the rest of their life. Unfortunately, teens have to reject everything their parents stand for so that they can figure out who they are and what they stand for. Teens are *internal* and *away from* their parents and *external* and *toward* their friends. To reduce conflict in the house, I started playing with language to motivate our daughter to clean her room. Here's the one that worked the best:

"*Don't think* about how nice your room will look after you've cleaned it and how much more time your friends

Questions & Answers

Ask: How do you know you:
- have done a good job?
- have a good relationship?
- have a good product?

Listen: I just know (internal)
People tell me (external)

Motivating Language

Internal (40%)	External (40%)
you might consider	experts say
you decide	over 1 million sold
look or read this	approved by

will want to spend with you." Since I said "don't think" she had to think about it. Then I painted a picture of a cleaned room and put her friends in it so that she would have something to move toward. An hour later the room was clean!

Questions

To find out if someone is internal (leader) or external (follower), you simply ask:

How do you know:
- you've done a good job?
- have a good marriage?
- bought the right car?

The answer will either be "I just know" or "people tell me." Internals often touch their chest or stomach to show you that the answer is *inside*. Externals will usually gesture *outside* their body to show that the decision is made for them externally.

Motivation

To motivate internal leaders, we have to offer them information and let them decide: "*You might consider* this model which comes with everything from the bare bones to a luxury edition, and *only you can decide* which options are right for you. Look over this information, then decide for yourself.

To motivate external people, we need to help them understand what other people think: "I want you to have this item because six other people on your block also found it a tremendous

Leader–Follower

"And I say you can afford it!"

value." "Over 1,000,000 copies sold!" Or say: "That's a good idea. Go for it."

When working with two or more people, it's a good idea to use both styles. To appeal to both simultaneously, we can use language that covers the gamut: "Thousands of people own this product, but only you can decide if it is right for you." Or as teens might say: "Everyone else's parents let them stay out past 12, but you know best."

Internal (40%)	External (40%)
You might consider...	Doctors recommend...
Here's the information...	Approved by...
Only you can decide...	Experts say...

According to the research, 40% of people will be internal in any situation, 40% will be external, and 20% will be able to do both. This means that you might consider adjusting your language to match your audience so that you can create deeper rapport and motivate them more easily, without alienating anyone.

Leaders

As a leader or manager, you might consider that 60% of your employees will be external. So you might consider giving everyone positive feedback about their performance, because the externals will thrive on it and the internals will use it as information to confirm their own opinions. Otherwise, the externals will feel unsure of their contribution and nag you endlessly about their performance. And the internals will develop their own ideas about their performance which may or may not align with yours.

Leader

Follower

To speed up any decision making process, gather as much information as quickly as possible. Talk to people, read reports, and do whatever is necessary to get to a level of confidence in your decision.

Followers

As an external, recognize that you need to carefully select the people you ask for help. Ask experts, not just anyone. When I write a book, I want feedback from other writers, not unskilled family members.

Presentations to a Group

When presenting to an audience or group, always assume that the group is both *internal* and *away from* you. In the first 60 seconds people decide whether to listen or not based on your credibility and connection. So in those opening 120 words consider using *internal* and *away from* influencing language:

> *"Today I'd like to offer some ideas that* you might consider *about how to avoid* these consequences *and receive* these benefits. *Only you can decide* which ones are right for you.*"*

Marketing and Sales

Externals are the easiest to motivate to buy. Just give them the testimonials of experts or, as a friend, simply recommend a solution. They'll buy. Internals need enough facts and information (including testimonials) to make a proper evaluation of a product or service. Make sure you feed them all the data they need *before* they make the decision, because it's hard to change afterwards.

Chapter 5

Innovator-Processor

As I've mentioned before, when my wife and I come home on Friday night, the whole conversation usually goes like this:

"*What do you want to do?*" I ask. (*External*)

"I don't know, *what do you want to do?*" she replies.

"Well, we could go to a movie *or* we could go out to eat," I say. (*Options/toward*)

She says: "Well, I *wouldn't* want to see anything too violent and I *wouldn't* want to eat too much." (*Away*)

"We could go see the new romantic comedy, *or* we could go eat a Piccolos," I reply. (*Options/toward*)

"Why *don't* we do to the movie *and then* go out to eat." (*Procedures*)

Innovator–Processor

If you follow all the rules, you miss all the fun.
-Katharine Hepburn

There is always one best way of doing things.
 -Emerson

Options–Procedures

Options people need choices, but if you have trouble deciding or you hesitate because there might be a better option, limit yourself to three alternatives and pick one. Do you have a hard time completing projects? Following a recipe is another way to accomplish your goals.

Procedures people like routine, habit, process and procedure. Do you have problems when a familiar routine stops working or doesn't work in a certain circumstance? Develop a procedure to follow when your processes break down or stop working. Develop a process to deal with the unexpected.

The first two lines show that we are both *external* to each other, which makes it hard to make a decision. Then I offer two general *options*: eat out *or* go to a movie. She responds in *away from* language about what she wants to avoid. I respond with two more specific *options* which meet her criteria. Then she responds with a *process* for sequencing the two options. (Understanding our language differences probably saved our marriage.)

So far, we've covered *toward-away* and *internal-external*. The next motivation program involves *options* and *procedures*.

If I asked you a question like: "Why did you choose your current job or relationship?" would you tend to respond with a list of criteria–reasons *why* you chose your current job, or a story about *how* you got the job?

• **Options** people give a list of criteria– challenging, flexible, freedom, etc. Their answers often sound like a smorgasbord of possibilities. Options people can answer this "why" question easily. Options people, by their nature, spend so much time on finding all of the options that they have a hard time finishing tasks. They like choices.

• **Procedures** people can't answer a "why" question. They answer the question: "How did you get your current job?" They tell a chronological, step-by-step story. Processors can follow a process, but can stumble when the process no longer works. When the market changes, you need to adapt to it.

Questions & Answers

Ask: Why did you choose your
current job? Relationship?
Product? Service?

Listen: • Series of words or short
phrases (options)
• Story about how you got the
job, relationship, or product
(procedures)

Motivating Language

Innovator	Processor
alternatives	step-by-step
options	process
freedom	procedure
break the rules	the "right" way

Think of jobs where processes have to be followed rigorously--airline mechanics, nursing, radiology, or running a fast food restaurant. Would you hire someone who is *options-* or *procedures-oriented*? In jobs where consistency is essential, procedures people are a good choice because they enjoy following a process.

Now imagine a job like leading a high-tech company, inventing things, reducing costs, reinventing a process, or just making improvements. Would you want options or procedures? Changing the world requires options thinking, but we can't stop there. To think up the change is one thing, but to deploy it is another. Many high tech companies have failed because the founder was a great options thinker, but failed to implement procedures to ensure continued success.

In a business relationship, these two opposites can drive each other crazy unless they recognize the benefit each provides. Research and development often drives manufacturing crazy with each new enhancement. The options thinker imagines new ways of doing things and the procedures person can figure out how to implement them. Together, they are a powerful team.

Motivation

Options people say: "So what are our choices?" "Have we investigated all of the available alternatives?" Motivate them by offering "what" to do and let them figure out "how" to do it. "We need to deliver our service in half the time." Options people like to break the rules.

Procedures people say: "What's our plan?" "What's the next step?" Motivate them by creating a specific plan or giving them step-by-step instructions. Avoid giving them choices. Because unless you tell them how to move forward, they can get stumped. Procedures people like to do the right things the right way.

Marketing

Once aware of this pattern, you'll begin to see and hear it in modern advertising:

Outback Steakhouse: *No rules*, just *right*.

Oppenheimer Funds: The *right way* to invest.

How can you, like Outback Steakhouse, use this language pattern to frame your product or service as both an option *and* a procedure? Could Oppenheimer Funds reach more clients by saying: "The *right way* to invest from a *variety* of funds.

Careers and Hiring

As you might imagine, this motivation program is critical to success and happiness in a career. A procedural person will be miserable in an innovator's job and vice versa. Which one are you or can you do both?

When it comes to hiring the right person for a job, you need to figure out if they will be required to mainly do procedural or variable tasks. Then hire appropriately. Because we feel comfortable with people who are like us, innovators tend to hire other innovators and processors tend to hire more procedural people. To create and develop a more productive team, match people to the job they are hired to do, not to the way you think.

Chapter 6

Doer-Thinker

Ever known someone who seems to think or talk endlessly about doing things without ever actually doing them? As a doer in many situations I find this frustrating. My wife will talk endlessly about a home improvement, but rarely jump into action. I eventually get tired of listening to her talk and just do it. Then, of course, she starts talking about a different improvement. Sometimes she'll mention something she wants me to do before the end of the day and I'll start doing it. Surprised at my action she'll say, "you don't have to do it right now." On the other hand, I thought about this book for several years before I nudged myself into action.

Doer–Thinker

Things do not get better by being left alone.
-Winston Churchill

Active–Passive

Active people don't have any trouble getting right into it. So, "just do it."

Passive people keep waiting for a stimulus. Ask yourself: "Haven't I waited long enough? Or am I just going to keep putting it off? What will it cost me if I wait?" In the Peanuts cartoon strip, Charlie Brown still hasn't spoken to the little red-haired girl, and it's been decades.

In some situations a person can be an active doer and in others the same person can ponder, think, discuss, and consider taking action for a long time. My wife's grandmother came across America in a covered wagon. From the time she retired at the age of 65 until her death in her 90s she talked about writing a book about her experiences as a young girl on a wagon train–stories her family would have cherished.

So this motivation program will determine if you jump into action or if you need some prodding to take action. This motivation program has been described as active-passive or proactive-reactive.

If someone asks you: "What do you want in a job? do you answer: "I want to be able set my own objectives and schedules." or do you answer: "I want my boss to tell me what is required and I'll get it done." Are you a "self-starter" or a "kick-starter"?

Business Applications

In the workplace, there are jobs that call for either active and passive motivations. A salesperson has to be active to make sales calls. A passive-orientation might be ideal for processing incoming calls, correspondence, or orders–the arrival of an order triggers the processing of it. Just as a passive person might be miserable in sales, an active person might be bored processing orders.

In a business relationship, do you think that actives and passives understand each other? Probably not. Which one tends to get more rewards and recognition? Which one feels undervalued? But consider that a salesperson probably couldn't survive without the people who process

Questions & Answers

Ask: What do you want in a job?
            Tell me about a time when
            you really got things done.
Listen: doing (active)
            reacting (passive)

Motivating Language

Active (20%)	Passive (20%)
Just do it	• Haven't you waited long enough? • Consider, then do it.

the sales orders and deliver the goods. Success in most endeavors involves using all of the motivation styles to optimize the outcome.

If someone asked you: "What do you want in a personal relationship?" Would you reply: "I want someone who's willing to go after everything we want in life." or do you reply: "I want a relationship where I can fully support whatever it is we decide to do." This motivation style can have profound affects on a couple's experience.

20 percent of people will be active *doers* in any given situation; 20 percent will be passive thinkers; and 60% will do some of both: thinking then acting. For the majority in the middle this is often their strategy: consider, then act. For example, I like to research major purchases before I buy. I'll read Consumer Reports or internet reviews before I take action. But once I decide, the action follows almost immediately. I don't have to have anyone nudge me into action.

Unlike the other motivation programs, there aren't any ideal questions you can ask that will determine where someone is active or passive. The real test is in their behavior. Do they "just do it" or do they have to "think about it" and finally be "told to do it?" In your own life, think about the things you jump into doing without a lot of thought. Now consider the things you tend to analyze, study, and ponder before taking action. It might be investing for retirement or writing a book. Most people have certain aspects of their life that make them hesitate, but haven't you waited long enough to start taking some action in these areas of your life, or are you going to wait until it's too late?

Passive

*"We used to call Ferguson 'lazy' --
but now it's 'motivationally impaired.'"*

Active language involves statements of what is going to be done. Active people might say: "Consider it done." "Let's make it happen." To motivate an active person is easy, say: "Here's what's needed...how soon can you have it done?"

Passive language involves questions about what to do and how to do it. Passives might ask: "What do you want me to do?" To motivate a passive, say:

"Haven't you waited long enough to start this project? "What will it cost you if you wait any longer?"

"Are you fed up enough to want to do something about this or do you want to wait until it gets even worse?"

"You're tired of waiting, aren't you?"

Doers don't take much encouragement to get them going, but passives often do. So haven't you waited long enough to start helping the thinkers in your life accomplish their dreams. Don't think about the remorse they will feel later in life having wasted all those precious years thinking, when they could have been doing something to achieve their goals.

Marketing

Marketing to *active* people isn't that hard. If they're *internal* you give them information and ask them to act. If they're *external*, you show how they'll be joining an elite group supported by experts in the field.

Marketing to *passive* people requires a little more attention. Use phrases like "for a limited time only" to compel them to stop thinking and start doing. Limit the number of classroom seats or products available to create a sense of *scarcity* that will trigger action. "After all, haven't you waited long enough to own your own home, car, stereo, cell phone?"

Teams

Teams can get into trouble if they don't have any active doers on the team. Compare an effective team with another that wasn't. What was the difference? In some teams, conflict among various motivation programs will stop a team, but in other teams, there isn't an active leader. I worked with one reengineering team that did a beautiful redesign, but couldn't get started on the actual business change. I suggested to the VP to get an active, procedural doer to lead the implementation and the project took off.

Hiring

Everyone seems to want to hire *active* go-getters, but aren't there positions which require a *reactive* or *passive* strategy? Answering the phone, customer care, repair, and maintenance are just a few of the jobs that are triggered into action by an external force. Match the right people to the right job and you'll have a highly productive workforce.

Personal

Take a moment to examine your own life. In what areas of your life are you *active*? You know, where you get things done easily and quickly.

Now in what areas are you more *passive* or *reactive?* Simply recognizing these areas is the first step to becoming more resourceful. Set time limits for taking action on these delayed projects. Consider what you'll lose if you don't start taking action now. You've waited long enough; isn't it time to get started now?

Chapter 7

Evolutionary-
Revolutionary

I worked for the phone company at the time of the Bell System breakup. The monopoly was being asked to compete. It turned out to be a trying time, because the local phone company was being asked to change from a provider of POTS–plain old telephone service–into a competitive supplier of communications, information, and entertainment. After years of providing the same old service, the company was being asked to provide new, more innovative and better services. Unfortunately, the company had selectively hired people who liked the status quo. A decade later after rounds of downsizing, the phone

Evolutionary– Revolutionary

Response To Change

Evolutionaries like to improve things. Find a way to make things better in your job or relationship. This is the essence of the Six Sigma, quality improvement movement.

Revolutionaries like to tear down the old and replace it with the newest ideas, technologies, etc. Instead of changing everything, find out what small change will produce the biggest impact. This is the essence of reengineering and innovation.

Fundamentalists like everything to stay the same. Find ways to see the similarities between coming changes and the current state of affairs. Fundamentalists are prime candidates for Darwin Awards.

companies were caught unaware by the sudden growth of "wireless" communications and the internet's demands for high-speed, second lines for home computers. Corning Glass, which invented fiber optics in the 1960s, had a hard time interesting the phone companies in high speed fiber networks because no one needed that much bandwidth to carry person-to-person calls. Besides, the prevailing wisdom was that you needed copper wire, not fiber, to carry voice signals, and there was already so much invested in copper. While perfectly positioned to be the internet communications solution for the country, most telephone companies hesitated to build these new, high speed networks, allowing smaller, faster, more innovative competitors to grab this high end market. Most hesitated to build wireless communications systems, as well. This story encapsulates the essence of the fifth motivation style–response to change:

- **difference** people are paradigm "shifters" who change the rules and patterns that formerly succeeded. Consider the digital clock vs the mechanical clock; the personal computer vs the mainframe. These revolutionaries like to initiate major changes in their life every 18-24 months. They represent about 30% of the population. In what area of your life are you driven to change every 1-2 years?

- **progress** people are paradigm "pioneers" who take the paradigm shift and begin to extend and enhance it. Compare an early Intel 8086 computer chip with only 27,000 transistors to a Pentium chip with over 9

Questions & Answers

Ask: What is the *relationship* between your job this year and last year?

Listen: • Same, similar (Same)
           • Better, more (Progress)
           • There is no relationship. (Difference) Do you mean "What's the *difference*?"

Motivating Language

Sameness	Progress	Difference
same	improve	new
similar	enhance	different
familiar	better	breakthrough

million! These evolutionaries like to initiate major changes in their life every 5-7 years. They represent 65% of the population.

- **sameness** people are the paradigm "settlers" who arrive after it's been proven perfectly safe to do so. These fundamentalists only initiate major changes in their life every 15-25 years. They represent the remaining 5% of the population.

One of the greatest areas for conflict in business or relationships is our individual response to change. Some people thrive on change, others prefer incremental improvements, and still others want everything to stay the same. Sameness people, companies, and ideologies have a hard time adapting to changes in their environment as the phone company story demonstrates.

Progress people can take any product or process and begin to make it better. America found this out in the 70s and 80s. American companies created lots of new products, but the Japanese companies rapidly improved and enhanced the designs to quickly meet the varied needs of consumers. In grade school, students learn about the American Revolution and embody much of this entrepreneurial spirit, but they may not be as effective at improving, expanding or enhancing products as other cultures, because of the overriding metaphor of revolution and independence.

Difference people are always looking for the next breakthrough. They often change the "paradigms" or existing rules in a given industry. In a phone company resistant to changes in the status quo, difference-oriented

Evolutionary

"...and just exactly what is the 'and much, much more' mentioned in your ad?"

Revolutionary

"There goes the neighborhood."

leaders started moving into other lines of business: real estate, financial business...almost anything except the core business. Most of these businesses have now been sold and the capital funneled back into wireless or high-speed internet communications.

Current business books suggest that you need to "lead the revolution" while others tout "breakthrough improvement," but consider that all businesses rely on some combination of these three patterns. All businesses succeed by following procedures and routine, but they also need some element of innovation and improvement to stay competitive. Unions are mainly sameness. R&D departments are mainly difference.

In a relationship, one spouse will want to keep the house the same, while the other will continually redecorate. A parent may want their child to look "normal" while the teen may change their hair style or clothing every few months.

Motivation

To influence a *sameness* person, we must discover how the change is the same or similar to what they already know or do. To influence a *progress* person, we must show how it's an improvement. To influence a *difference* person, we must highlight how it's new and different. *And* do all three for any *group* of people.

Sameness: This is *similar* to the way you've always done it, so it should be *familiar*.

Progress This incorporates several *improvements* and *enhancements* that will prove invaluable.

Difference: This *breakthrough* strategy is *new*.

Corporate Change

Progress is a nice word. But change is its motivator. And change has its enemies.
-Robert F. Kennedy

All: This is *similar* to the way you've always done things with some useful *enhancements* and some totally *new* functionality.

Motivating Companies to Change

Successful change is the process by which:
1. an innovation
2. is communicated through certain channels
3. over time
4. among the members of a social system

The average period for the universal adoption of an innovation is 25 years. Question: "Is there a way to speed it up? Is there a way to make any change more contagious in your company?" I believe the answer is "Yes!" So I'd like to offer for your consideration some information about how contagious ideas spread, what we can learn from it, and how to apply it.

For over 50 years, researchers have studied how changes are adopted, adapted or rejected by societies and cultures. This research is described in *The Diffusion of Innovations*, by Everett Rogers (Free Press, 1995). Diffusion is a model for understanding social change. There are several characteristics of "innovations" that can be adjusted to increase the speed of adoption–*advantages, compatibility, complexity, trialability,* and *observability.* You might think of these characteristics as a way to develop rapport with any group of people that represent a culture–corporations, departments, etc. There is a clear decision strategy people follow when they decide to adopt, adapt, or reject an innovation. And there are various communication channels through which an innovation

Innovation

*The new always carries
with it the sense of
violation, of sacrilege.
What is dead is sacred;
what is new, that is,
different, is evil,
dangerous, or subversive.*
-Henry Miller

"infection" can spread, although the winner is one-to-one positive word of mouth. And the change agent (motivator) plays a key role in the speed of adoption.

I'd like you to consider that TQM and reengineering failed to take root in many companies because the implementation failed to apply the lessons learned about diffusion–how changes are adopted by society. Let's use this change model to filter our experience. Along the way I'll suggest some possible ways to adjust our approach to increase the spread of new, improved, and time tested ideas.

Characteristics of Innovations

The heart of any change is about doing business better, faster, and cheaper. By letting customers get what they want, when they want it, at a price they perceive as offering superior value, businesses thrive. TQM or reengineering, however, are often about preventing problems through improvement or redesign. Innovations involving prevention spread more slowly than innovations that solve pressing problems.

Compatibility - To be successful, any innovation must seek compatibility (i.e., similarity) with a culture's:

• values and beliefs
• previously introduced ideas
• "felt" needs

What can you do to make a change more compatible?

Complexity - the degree to which an innovation is perceived as difficult to understand and use (i.e., different). What can you do to reduce a change's perceived complexity?

Decision to Adopt

*To say yes, you have to
sweat and roll up your
sleeves and plunge both
hands into life up to the
elbows. It is easy to say
no, even if saying no
means death.*
-Jean Anouilh

Trialability - new ideas, tried on the installment plan are easier to adopt because you can learn by doing.

People like to try things and then decide. Most employees want to serve customers more effectively. What else can you do to increase an idea's trialability?

Observability - the ability to see results and for others to see them too. Notice this satisfies the motivation programs *internal* and *external*. Recommendation: Find a way to make the effects of improvements "visible" to casual observers.

So these are the characteristics that can make a change more contagious—advantages, compatibility, complexity, trialability, and observability. Now let's look at the decision process used to adopt, adapt, or reject an innovation and the various types of adopters.

The Innovation-Decision Process

There is a step-by-step process people follow to decide to adopt, adapt, or reject a change or innovation in their lives:

1. First comes **knowledge** - an awareness and understanding of the problem. This happens when a company decides to implement an improvement. This initial awareness always involves personal questions:

- What is the change?
- How-to apply the change? (Most important when trialing innovations.)
- Why? - reasons and values for making the change
- Where might it apply in your life?

2. Next comes **persuasion**. People need to be persuaded (i.e., motivated) to try the change. Using the

Adopter Categories

*The reasonable man
adapts to the world,
the unreasonable man
persists in trying to adapt
the world to himself*
George Bernard Shaw

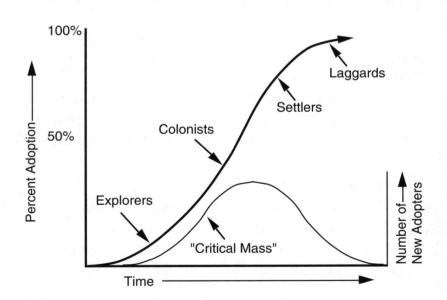

language skills of preceding chapters, learn to speak out of all sides of your mouth when presenting the change. How can you become the role model to influence more people to embrace a change in people, process, or technology?

3. Then comes the **decision**. Each person seeks information to decide (*internal*) whether to adopt or reject, either *passively* or *actively*, the change.

4. Then, assuming the person decides to adopt the change, they begin **implementation**. This sometimes requires adaptation (i.e., *improvement*) of the change (e.g., applying the change in a context of interest).

5. Finally, after a period of time or a number of trials, people achieve **confirmation** (*convincer strategy*). They confirm for themselves that the change is a good one and that it deserves to stay. Or, they may decide to reject the change.

This decision process becomes increasingly complex when working with a system, group or organization rather than one individual, because of varying adopters.

Adopter Categories

Innovators (Venturesome explorers)–they are the active seekers of *new* and *different* ideas. They are intuitive (they depend on *internal* knowing not external information, because the facts to back up the choice usually aren't available yet). Often perceived as deviant from the social system. A few become opinion leaders (champions) of the innovation.

Early Adopters (Respectful Colonists)–they are quick to notice shifts. Also *internal*, they begin to imple-

Accelerating Change

Adapt or perish, now as ever, is Nature's inexorable imperative.
-H. G. Wells

ment and *improve* on the paradigm shift. Early adopters are evolutionaries. Sales people (motivators) are essential for early adopters.

Early Majority (Deliberate Settlers)–these people rely on the early adopters and opinion leaders–centers of influence–to decide to adopt (*external*). They need a coach.

Late Majority (Skeptical Settlers)–These people won't adopt until it's safe (*away from*). Neighbors from the early majority are important for later adopters (*external*).

Laggards (Traditional)–These people can be every bit as influential as the early adopters. In businesses, laggards are the corporate *immune system*, they try to *prevent* a new idea from spreading (*away from*). They want things to stay the *same*. A gentle, non-threatening introduction of changes with early adopters will avoid triggering the immune response.

Speed of Adoption

The speed of adoption can be improved by how it is done and who has the authority to make it happen. The adoption decisions (in order of speed of adoption):

Speed	Type
Fastest:	**Optional**–choices made by each individual (e.g., participation in the change)
Medium:	**Authority**–made by one or a few people with power, status, or technical expertise.
Slowest:	**Collective**–made by consensus of members
Varies:	**Combination** of the above.

Change Agents

The greatest response to change agent effort occurs when opinion leaders adopt, which usually occurs somewhere between 3 and 16 percent adoption.
-Everett Rogers

Communication Channels

A communication channel carries messages. It determines how information travels from one person to another.

Mass Media: TV, radio, and print can:
1. Reach large audiences
2. Create and spread information
3. Change weakly held attitudes

Interpersonal Channels

These are a slower but more effective means of persuading people to adopt a new idea. Used in the persuasion stage, it can:
1. Provide two-way exchange of information.
2. Allow an individual to form or change strongly held attitudes or beliefs (Chapter 9).

Change Agent Role

What is your role in getting people to adopt a change? How can you make it more contagious?
1. *Prevent* too much "adoption" (i.e., adoption by laggards–people who might reject it or delay implementation) which, paradoxically, will speed up diffusion.
2. Develop the need for change (*toward-away*)
3. Exchange information (*internal-external*)
4. Diagnose problems (*away from*)
5. Create an intent in the employees to change (*toward*)
6. Translate that intent into action (*active*)
7. Stabilize and sustain the adoption (*progress*)
8. Achieve self-renewing behavior.

Speaking to Groups

When speaking to a group of two or more people, assume that all of the motivation programs exist in your audience. That means that you will need to speak out of all sides of your mouth using all of the motivation language: *toward-away, internal-external, options-procedures, passive-active,* and *sameness-progress-difference.* Each part of your audience will selectively hear what they want to hear making it easier for them to adopt the change. Because it's easier to hear messages coded in their preferred motivation style, the people in your audience hear what is meant for them and ignore the rest.

Conclusions

Over 50 years of research has shown how to accelerate the adoption and application of changes through:

1. better presentation of the perceived attributes of the change. Use the language tools in preceding chapters to reach all of your audience.

2. understanding decisions and their effect on adoption

3. the power of mass media and personal communications

4. the change agent's role

To expand the impact of a change, you might need to begin to craft your communications in ways that invite the early majority to participate in the transformation. Only you can decide if this flexibility of choice is right for you, and how soon you can bring your remarkable talents to bear on the needs of our "global village."

Chapter 8

Dreamer-Realist-Critic

In any high performance team–business, family, or marriage–there are always dreamers, realists, and critics. This chapter explores additional ways to motivate each one.

- **Dreamers** are more *toward, options, difference.* They are also more *visual, big picture,* and *future-*oriented.

- **Realists** are more *toward, internal, procedures, active,* and *progress.* They are also more *detail-*oriented and firmly rooted in the *present.*

- **Critics** are more *away from, difference,* and *internal.* They are also able to use *big picture-detail, past-future* to make comparisons and evaluate the possible consequences and failures of any activity.

Visionary–Realist

*Hindsight is useful for
sharpening your
foresight.*
Peter Schwartz

Big Picture–Detail

Visionaries easily grasp the whole situation.
They like to think top down. They like the
view from 30,000 feet.

Realists like the nitty-gritty, nuts-and-bolts of
things. They like to think bottom up. They
like having both feet on the ground. Realists
like to live in the present..

Big Picture-Detail

One of the most important patterns in visually-oriented people is big picture-detail.

Big picture people are dreamers and visionaries. They like to see the whole panorama of possibilities, understand the broad scope of an issue before they get into the details. They actively resist getting into the details before they understand the global nature of the issue they are addressing. Big picture people get into trouble by constantly expanding the scope of a project. They can focus on the details of turning the big picture into reality.

Detail people are implementors and doers. They like to get a grip on the details first. They like to get in on the ground floor and understand everything as it builds up. Detail people can get into trouble by working hard in an area that is unrelated to the overall mission and direction. They can spend a lot of time toiling in the wrong fields. Detail people can learn to look up periodically to determine if they are on track or off course.

Goal achievement often relies on the ability to chunk large tasks down into smaller chunks. This is the special skill of detail people. People who have difficulty setting and achieving goals often benefit from learning how to segment projects into manageable tasks.

Time

"My, my you certainly do have your life planned out,
this resumé covers past <u>and</u> future."

Past-Present-Future

People too narrowly focused on the **past** have a hard time being in the present. They often miss the pleasures of today and fail to plan for their tomorrows. They may be considered out of touch, but they may enjoy history. Anyone can learn the mental skills of stepping into the future and living in the present.

People who live in the **present** moment will enjoy today. They may not, however, learn from their past or plan for their future. They can learn how to access the past and the future.

Future thinkers may spend all their time imagining the future and never really enjoy the fruits of their earlier planning. They can learn how to be present and use the past.

See-Hear-Feel

Seeing people use visual words in their language, words like: *see, clear, paint, picture, view*. Highly visual people include painters, architects, and graphic designers.

Hearing people use auditory words like: *hear, click, ring, sounds*, etc. Auditory people are often musical or lyrical in their use of language and sound.

Feeling people use kinesthetic words like *feel, touch, warming up, leaves me cold, grip, handle*, etc. Donald Trump, in *The Art of the Deal*, said that no matter how good a deal *looks* on paper, if it doesn't *feel right*, he won't do it. (His strategy: see-feel.) The best athletes also say they can *see* someone do something and *feel* how to do it in their body. There is very little internal chatter in top athletes.

Convincer Strategy

Ask:　How do you know if ...?
- someone has done a good job?
- a product works well?
- a company provides good service?

Listen:　seeing, hearing, reading, or doing

Ask:　How many times do you need to (see, hear, read, do) to become convinced?

Listen:　1, number, period of time, never

Motivation

Repeat for the number of times necessary in the optimal format for acceptance.

To motivate these types of people, you must first establish rapport. To more easily motivate visual people use colorful words. To motivate auditories, use musical words and tempo. To motivate kinesthetic people use words that have some weight to them. Seeing, hearing, and feeling words are powerful ways to create and build a connection with another person.

Convincing People

Ever notice that it takes people time to become convinced to do something, to take action, to adopt a change? People become convinced in three main ways:

- visual - seeing
- auditory - hearing, or reading
- kinesthetic - doing

Becoming convinced may happen instantaneously or it may take some time. There are four time frames to consider when attempting to convince someone:

- only once
- a number of times
- over a limited period of time
- every time

To find out how to convince someone, ask them a couple of questions:

How do you know if something is a good product? or How do you know if someone is good at their job?

The answer will typically be: "I see, hear, read, or do..."

Then ask: "How many times do you need to (see, hear, read, do) to become convinced? The answer will usually be one of the four above. Given their answer, you will know how many times you will need to present an idea and in what format you need to present it to be accepted.

One study at the Space Defense Command found that presentations in the target general's preferred mode increased productivity 2.5 times. When presented in a less preferred mode, the general typically asked for revisions and additional presentations to become convinced of the data's validity.

So how do they want to see, hear, read, or do it, and how many times? Traditional sales literature suggests that it may take up to seven visits to make a sale, but it may take far fewer if the information arrives in the form the client prefers.

Summary

There are many ways to create deep and lasting rapport that will allow you to more easily influence the people in your life. You might consider creating verbal rapport with seeing, hearing, and feeling words. Or you might expand or narrow the scope of your presentation. You might present your ideas in the manner your client prefers and just the right number of times. And you can tailor it to match their sense of time–past, present, or future.

Chapter 9

The Power of Beliefs

Beliefs have great power. They can let information in or shut it out. They can make you do stupid things or wildly beneficial ones. Beliefs provide both motivation and permission to behave in alignment with our beliefs. Most beliefs operate outside of your conscious awareness.

Most beliefs help you, but limiting beliefs can stop you from achieving your dreams and ambitions. Limiting beliefs often serve a positive purpose–safety, security, etc., but at a high cost of living a less than enjoyable life. All beliefs are formed, over time, through interaction with people and surroundings. It's difficult if not impossible to motivate someone to do something that conflicts with their beliefs.

Belief Shield

People cling to old beliefs, values, abilities, and identities, even at the expense of their well-being.

Belief   Belief

Shield   Shield

But here's the good news: Beliefs can be changed! By understanding each belief's:
- positive intention and benefits
- presuppositions or assumptions
- structure

Using these three elements of a belief, you can begin to expand, clarify, redefine, or retrain your mind and the minds of other people in ways that will change the belief from limiting to empowering.

Belief Shield

Beliefs are what Peter Senge, author of *The Fifth Discipline*, calls "mental models." Beliefs, like an invisible bubble or boundary shield, sift through all of the information you receive through your senses, keeping what's "true" (i.e., aligns with, supports and reinforces your beliefs) and rejecting what's "false" (i.e., conflicts with your beliefs). Beliefs are neither true nor false; they are simply mental filters that you have created to make daily life simpler. You can let them fall away like leaves from a tree or scales from a fish, and replace them with more useful, more invigorating beliefs.

Empowering Belief: Any belief can be changed. Exchange your limiting beliefs for more successful ones. Tune up your empowering beliefs to be more powerful.

Limiting Beliefs

Limiting beliefs are often created as an excuse to hide our lack of knowledge about how to do something–relating, being, doing, learning, getting, or having. There are five common limiting beliefs: hopeless, helpless, worthless, useless, and blameless. Their expansive coun-

Limiting Beliefs

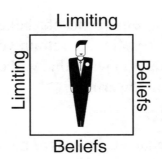

Limiting Beliefs	
Hopeless	Not possible
Helpless	Not capable
Worthless	Not worthy
Useless	Not desirable
Blameless	Not responsible

terparts are possible, capable, worthy, valuable, and responsible. Let's examine each one:

1. **It's hopeless** (i.e., it's not possible). Sometimes, faced with a seemingly insurmountable problem, we can take the easy way out by saying: "It's not possible; it's hopeless." Of course, when we say this, it immediately starts to block information to the contrary. We stop seeking the answers we need to solve whatever problem that confronts us. It doesn't matter if the issue is healing an illness, making a million dollars, or finding a mate, if we don't think it's possible, we just won't do what's necessary to make it happen. One of the most blatant of these is when a doctor gives a patient a "terminal" diagnosis; it's only "terminal" because *the doctor doesn't know how to cure it*, not because it's *incurable*. When a patient spontaneously recovers from a "terminal" disease, it's perceived as a "misdiagnosis" not a brilliant act of self-healing. Why aren't we more curious about how spontaneous remission occurs?

2. **I'm helpless** (i.e., I don't know how to do it). We have these big brains, but sometimes we don't have what I call the *KnowWare* to run them. It's like having a computer with a huge hard drive, but no application software. Or, we may know how to do something very similar in another situation, but we don't notice how to use it in a similar, but different situation. Some people, for example, find it easy to meet and talk to other people in a business context, but stammer and hesitate in a bar with the opposite sex.

Most of us have the mental software to handle most situations. (Here's an **empowering belief**: Everyone already has all the KnowWare they need.) But often we have

How Beliefs Form

compartmentalized that ability into a single context, place or time. So you might be great with unruly children, but not unruly co-workers or vice versa. To overcome the "know how" limitation, we can:

- discover what KnowWare we already have that can be enhanced to work in a new situation
- invoke our "learning" KnowWare to learn how to do something using books, tapes, seminars, and courses.

3. **I'm worthless** (i.e., I don't deserve success, love, happiness, etc.). Many ideologies pound this belief in from an early age. Parents, the earliest programmers, may deny children love or attention. Not in the spirit of harshness, but because of their own positive intentions and limitations. Remember, *your parents are running the KnowWare that they got from their parents*. It's hand-me-down, archaic code, so don't be surprised if some of it was limiting. It's the best they could do with what they had. From these repeated experiences, a child can create a belief that they aren't worthy.

There's a flip side to this belief: "I deserve, *because* I'm limited (incapable, helpless)." People are conditioned to believe that the world owes them something. One welfare recipient told me: "I deserve welfare, *because* I'm disabled." I asked, "How does being disabled actually mean that you are more employable?" Similarly, in relationships, people sometimes feel that "I deserve to have *you make me feel good*, because it means that you love me." (Don't you deserve to feel good about yourself anyway!)

Self-Fulfilling Prophesy

One-quarter to one-third of patients will improve if they merely <u>believe</u> they are taking effective medication.
-Bernie Siegel, M.D.

A man is what he believes.
- Anton Chekhov

4. **It's useless** (i.e., I don't want it). Invariably, this limitation comes from a misguided sense of values. We begin to believe that getting one thing *means* giving up something more important. For single people, getting married often seems to *mean* giving up their freedom. If we don't want something, we won't go after it.

This limitation is about an either/or decision: I can have either A or B (but not A *and* B). You can challenge this by asking: "How would getting A actually mean you can have more B?" How would being married actually give you more freedom? Remember, beliefs tend to blind us to other possibilities. They despise conflicting information.

Special Note: To motivate yourself and others you have to *want* to motivate them. You may not want some prospects as clients, so motivating them to buy would be counterproductive. You may not want to motivate your child to put a dirty shirt in the laundry.

5. **I'm blameless** (i.e., I'm not responsible) Patients turn over their health to doctors. Lovers turn over their happiness to their partners. Workers turn over job satisfaction to their managers. With this belief, people stop taking action to achieve their outcomes. They turn control over to someone else and *passively* wait for something to happen, then blame the other person if nothing does happen. Take control of your life, health, and happiness. (Better belief: I'm responsible for creating my life.)

One way this shows up in marriages is when one spouse makes the other miserable in an attempt to get the other person to initiate a divorce. That way, they are absolved of blame or guilt from the breakup of the marriage.

Edges of Possibility

Perhaps nobody ever accomplishes all that he feels lies in him to do, but nearly every one who tries his powers touches the walls of his being occasionally, and learns about how far to attempt to spring.
-Charles Dudley Warner

In a business, employees can make mistakes, offend co-workers, and act aggressively in an attempt to get fired from a job they don't like or enjoy. Again, to absolve themselves of blame for being fired. If their initial efforts to get fired don't work, they may escalate their behavior until it becomes dangerous, even fatal.

Common Limiting Beliefs

Spirit	• It's a sin, because a higher power would judge it so.

Identity	• I'm shy, lazy, not creative (characteristics)
	• I'm a victim of:
	  - my environment (present),
	  - childhood (past),
	  - internal demons (devil made me do it),
	  - external demons (others)

Beliefs	• Achieving success means *losing something more valuable.*
Values	• Getting married means giving up my freedom.
Capabilities	• I'm not good enough • I don't know enough • I can't get out of debt, poverty, this job, etc.
Environment	• Life is hard • You have to struggle to survive

Spin

We also make excuses for the way we behave because it's easier than changing behaviors. Some of the ways are:
  • Judging others is often a way to feel superior. Underlying judgements reflect beliefs. Examples: criticiz-

Convictions

Convictions are more dangerous enemies of truth than lies.
-Nietzsche

ing other drivers for slowness (my time is important) or bad driving (safety is important).

- Judgements of self—I'm not good enough, therefore I can't do something.
- Illusion of Safety—Limiting beliefs are like a cocoon that appear to keep us safe (It's not safe to be in a relationship), but actually prevent us from experiencing the fullness of life.
- Saves time and effort. "I'm not well" can cause others to take on more of your responsibilities.
- Generalizations about the past (In *Pretty Woman*, Julia Robert's character says, "I'm a bum magnet.")
- Generalizations from minimal evidence. Remember the convincer strategy? How many examples does it take to begin to form a belief...two or three?
- Distortions—turning opposing into supporting evidence
- Deletions—eliminating conflicting evidence
- Justification by imagining future results
- Self-fulfilling prophesy: belief causes action which reinforces the belief.

Changing Beliefs with Language

I've found "sleight of mouth" language patterns a powerful antidote for limiting beliefs. The great thing about them is that they can be used in everyday conversation with co-workers and family members.

Beliefs always take the linguistic form of:

"A *means* B" or "A *causes* B" or "I'm B *because* of A."

For example, "Being late, *means* you don't love me. Being late *makes* me think you don't love me. You don't

Sleight of Mouth

*Sleight of Mouth
patterns help people
enrich their
perspective, expand
their maps of the world
and reconnect with
their experience.*
-Robert Dilts

love me *because* you're always late." In this case, the behavior–being late–means or causes the person to feel unloved. You can imagine how someone who feels unworthy might take even these simple actions as evidence that they are worthless.

Transforming Limiting Beliefs

To gather the information you need to transform the belief using simple conversation, ask,

What's the opposite of A? Then ask:
What's the opposite of B?

Example: What's the opposite of being late? *Being on time.* What's the opposite of not loving you? *Caring about me.* Notice that what you think might be the opposite may not be what the other person holds in their mind as the opposite.

Now that you know the limiting belief and the opposites of A and B, ask the person each of the following questions. The belief will usually shift completely:

How would A actually mean/cause [opposite of B]?
How would [opposite of A] actually mean/cause B?
How would A actually mean/cause *not* B?
How would *not* A actually mean/cause B?
How would *not* A actually mean/cause *not* B?

How would <u>being late</u> actually mean I <u>care about you</u>?
How would <u>being on time</u> actually mean I <u>don't love you</u>?
How would <u>being late</u> actually mean <u>I love you</u>?
How would <u>not being late</u> actually mean I <u>don't love you</u>?
How would <u>not being late</u> actually mean I <u>don't care</u>?

Intelligence

The greatest intelligence is precisely the one that suffers most from its own limitations.
-Andre Gide

Example 2: "Falling off a bike means I'm clumsy."
A = Falling off a bike
B = I'm clumsy
Opposite of **A**: riding effortlessly
Opposite of **B**: coordinated

How would falling off a bike actually mean you're coordinated?
I didn't hurt myself when I fell. Even the best riders sometimes fall.
When would riding effortlessly actually mean you're clumsy?
When falling would prevent greater injury.
How would falling off a bike actually mean you're not clumsy?
It might mean I'm pushing the envelope, learning what I can do.
How would not falling off a bike actually mean you're clumsy?
When falling would prevent greater injury.
How would not falling off a bike actually mean you're not clumsy?
It would mean I've learned how to ride well.

Many people have a limiting belief that "doing it wrong means I'm stupid." It's difficult to motivate someone to do something if they believe they are bad, stupid or dumb about it. Empowering belief: I learn something from everything I do. Ask: "How does doing it wrong accelerate your learning?

This linguistic pattern helps create multiple points of view from which the limiting belief becomes more pliable

Limits

We expect more of ourselves than we have any right to, in virtue of our endowments.
-Oliver Wendell Holmes, Sr.

and open to reinterpretation. Limiting beliefs often take the following forms:

Limiting Beliefs	Core Value	Reason
It's not possible to...	relate	because _____.
I can't...	be	because _____.
I don't deserve to...	do	because _____.
I dont want to...	learn	because _____.
I'm not responsible...	get/have	because _____.

Benefit	Equals	Greater Cost
Getting what I want...		giving up _____.
Learning...		forgetting _____.
Doing...	means	losing _____.
Being...		abandoning _____.
Relating...		letting go of _____.

Limiting Belief:

Achieving success means giving up _____.
"Achieving success means selling my soul."
"Getting married means giving up my friends."
"Doing this job is a waste of time."

Shifting Beliefs Example

How would achieving success actually mean getting more _____?

How would *not* achieving success actually mean giving up more _____?

How would giving up _____ actually mean not getting success?

How would not giving up ____actually mean getting more success?

Once we know the structure and content of a person's belief, we can begin to shift it using sleight-of-mouth

Belief

A firm belief attracts facts. They come out of holes in th' ground an' cracks in th' wall to support belief, but the run away fr'm doubt.
-Finchley Peter Dunne

Loosening Beliefs

Sometimes, we need to loosen a person's hold on a belief so that we can start to shift it using the words *seems or appears:* So, for you it *seems* like getting success means giving up _____. (This statement presupposes that not everyone sees it the same way.)

Shifting Outcomes

Sometimes we have to shift the person's attention away from what they might lose to a more useful outcome: How would getting success mean *having more to give?*

Reframing

Sometimes we have to expand or narrow the focus of belief to get a shift. Expand to include more time, people, or situations, or narrow to focus on fewer people, situations or time. Or shift from short-term to long-term: How would achieving success make *your whole life better?* How would achieving success make *each day better?*

Intention

Sometimes it helps to draw people's attention to the positive intention of their belief, and move their attention off the limitation.

Belief: "Success means giving up time with my spouse."

So it's important to *sustain and enrich your marriage.* How would success make it *even easier to spend more quality time with your family and friends?*

Redefine

Sometimes we can redefine what either A or B would mean to the person:

Empowering Belief

The belief that becomes truth for me...is that which allows me the best use of my strength, the best means of putting my virtues into action
-Andre Gide

"I'm *afraid* achieving success would *take too long*."

So you're *concerned* that success would take *more time than you're willing to commit to it.* You're going to use that time one way or another; why not use it to achieve success?

Notice that we can change a word like *afraid* and soften it to *concerned*, thereby redefining and reframing the meaning. Consider the words: successful, wealthy, and *filthy* rich. The implications are vastly different. These shifts are the essence of what the media calls "spin."

Chunking

Ever noticed how some people like the view from 30,000 feet (big picture) and others want to bring the discussion back down to earth (detail)? To shift a belief, you can shift up to a more general, down to a more specific, or across to a similar, yet different point of view. Almost everyone who has difficulty succeeding has a hard time with the word, *selling*. The most common form of people's limiting belief is:

"Selling means manipulation."

Chunk up: Selling means helping people get what they want.

Chunk up: Selling means solving customer problems.

Chunk down: Selling means asking questions to verify the customer needs what we offer.

Chunk across: Selling means planting seeds to grow long-term relationships.

Counterexample

Sometimes a single example that runs counter to the limiting belief will change it. This is especially true when the belief involves words like *all* or *none*, *always*, or *never*, *everyone* or *no one*.

"I'll *never* succeed."

Never? You've never succeeded at anything? You survived your birth. You breathe, you eat, you walk.

Apply to Self

Another way to attack a belief is with its own language:

"You can't *trust* people."

So you can't *trust* what you just said?

That's not a very *trusting* thing to say.

Intention

The goal of these sleight-of-mouth patterns is to change:

Problems	into	Solutions
Failure	into	Learning
Impossibility	into	Possibility

Summary

The five limiting beliefs: hopeless, helpless, worthless, useless, and blameless can inhibit motivation. They often involve one of the five core values: people, places, activities, knowledge or things. Beliefs can form through accumulation, erosion, or trauma. They can be changed verbally by playing with the belief's structure and content using sleight of mouth.

Chapter 10

Creating Desire

In 1960, John F. Kennedy was president. ABC's Wide World of Sports was spanning the Globe. And in the small town of Graz, Austria, the 13-year old son of a local policeman sat in the only movie theatre in town. It was a cavernous old theater. Up on the screen was *Hercules Unchained*, one of the many Hercules movies starring Steve Reeves or Reg Park, two of the great body builders of the 1950s. As these scantily clad muscle men fought on the screen, the teenager decided to design his destiny. He said to himself: **"I can be there "** and he saw himself on the screen, felt his muscles rippling under the rough texture of the toga.

In this moment, he composed his master plan: He would move to America, become the world's greatest

Designing The Future

Extraordinary people live their lives backward. They stand in their future and determine how they would like their life to be. This vision of their future gives them a way to be in the present, and their actions spring naturally from this sense of who they are. Ordinary people simply live their past over and over again.

-Fred Shoemaker

body builder, and, by the age of 30, star in his first movie and be a millionaire. Now many people have great dreams, but he began to make his more real. He read body building magazines. Can you imagine him in his room, trying out all of the various poses? "Feels fantastic!" What if his mother had come in and said: "Arnold, Vat are you doing? Forget this silly nonsense. You are going to grow up, get a job, get married, and have children, just like your father." But she didn't. Both his parents supported what his unconventional career choice.

Imagine what happened when he discovered that body builders shave and oil their bodies before competitions.He probably locked himself in the family bathroom, snapped on a pair of Speedos, grabbed his father's safety razor and started shaving the soft hair on his legs. When he was done, he'd lather himself in baby oil, smelling it, feeling it on his skin. Posing before the tiny bathroom mirror. In this way, he began to make the future so real, so familiar that it was only a matter of time before he would succeed.

We know a lot about this man who became known as the Austrian Oak. Five years later, he won the Mr. Europe title. He would win five Mr. Universe and seven Mr. Olympia contests. He would marry into the Kennedy family and become one of the highest paid actors in the world.

There's nothing more motivating than a compelling future. And I know something about each person reading this book. At some point in your life, just like Arnold, you heard THE CALL of your destiny. You may have seen someone, heard someone, read a story or been

Destiny

touched in some way, but in that moment you knew exactly what you wanted to be. Most of you, however, didn't take the time to build a rich, 3-D experience of that future so that you knew what it was like before you arrived. So now I want you to begin to design your destiny and experience it now.

First, look out into your future, which for most of you is off to your right or out in front of you. See a role model, standing there waiting for you in your future. In your mind's eye travel out and step into their body. Snap them on like an ability suit. Feel what it's like to be in their clothes and skin. Look around you. Notice what you see, what it feels like, listen to the sounds around you, smell the air. Where are you? Who are you with? What are you doing? What are you learning? What do you own or have?

Now come back into the present and realize that this is just the little beginning of what you can do to enrich your mental maps of the future. You can do this in your mind or physically walk out into your future and experience it again and again, each time more fully. Each night as you dream, your unconscious can enrich this map even more. And as you design your future, it will become so real that it will carry you beyond your wildest dreams.

Schwartzenegger Strategy

Arnold's strategy uses the following steps:
1. See someone already "where you want to be," a role model. Say to yourself: "I can be there."
2. Step into your role model and feel what it feels like to already be there.
3. Repeat daily until you feel a sense of calm, like you're already there.

Design Your Destiny

*The winds and waves
are always on the side of
the ablest navigators*
-Edward Gibbon

Remove Your Barriers and Design Your Destiny

1. **Intention** - set your intent to transcend some limitation or achieve some desired outcome. Make it a 3-dimensional experience that engages all five senses–sight, sound, smell, taste, touch. Who else is there? What you doing?

2. **Action** - start taking steps to resolve the limitation or to move toward the desired objective. Make sure the steps are small enough that they can be done easily.

3. **Review** - assume that *everything is feedback.* What can you learn from each step of your journey?

4. Take action to close the gap between where you are and where you want to be.

5. Stay hungry: set new limits, raise the bar, set new thresholds or standards for excellence.

So what stops people from achieving their destiny? In some situations, people stop themselves by thinking about the time and effort involved in achieving their outcome. Or they may not have any *desire* for the objective. As one person put it: "Fat cats don't hunt." To get motivated, each person needs to get hungry for an outcome that would benefit them personally as well as the community around them.

In most cases, motivation comes from our desire to get from where we are now to where we want to be. To do this, you need to be able to:

1. Experience the end result (see, hear, feel, taste, and smell it with all your senses.)
2. Feel good about achieving the result
3. If the task is large or long, ask yourself what piece you can do *right now* in the time available.
4. Trigger yourself into action ("Just do it!")

Industry Futures

In the *Art of the Long View*, Peter Schwartz describes Shell Oil's planning process. Futurists call this "having your radar out." To anticipate and design the future, teams of managers can gather together and develop "scenarios" for each of the following possibilities:

- Optimistic - best possible outcome (toward)
- Status Quo - everything stays the same
- Pessimistic - worst possible outcome (away)

Teams can begin with big, high level world scenarios and then narrow their focus down to specific situations.

Designing the Future

The following series of questions have been designed to help you create a detailed internal map of a desired future.

1. Think about your future now. What do you truly want?
2. How will you know when you've achieved it? What will you see, hear, feel? Who will you be? What will you do?
3. Where, when, and with whom do you want this future?
4. What will having it do for you that's even more important?
5. In what ways have you already demonstrated that you have some of what you want?
6. As you think about it now, what resources—beliefs, values, capabilities, and behaviors—do you already have that will take you in the direction that you want to go?
7. Who is a ideal model for the type of person you want to become? Where can you learn more about them, study and learn their skills, abilities, beliefs, and values?
8. What skills will you need to accelerate your journey?
9. What's the first small step you need to take?

Haven't you waited long enough to embrace more of what's possible and to avoid the consequences of an unfulfilled life? Only you can decide to take the right steps to achieve your destiny. So learn how to ecologically and ethically motivate yourself and others. Bring your originality and uniqueness to healing and nurturing the world you live in.

Appendix A–Questions, Answers, and Motivation

Values - What's important to you about...?

Answer: power words and phrases

Toward-Away - Why is that important?

	Toward	**Away**
Answer:	get/have	not lose, wouldn't
Motivation	achieve goal	avoid consequences

Internal-External -
How do you know you've done a good job?

	Internal	**External**
Answer:	I just know.	People tell me.
Motivation:	You might consider	Experts say...

Options-Procedures -
Why did you choose your current job?

	Options	**Procedures**
Answer:	short phrases	tells a story
Motivation	choice	step-by-step
	freedom	process

Response to Change - What's the relationship between your job this year and last year?

	Sameness	**Progress**	**Difference**
Answer:	same	improved	new
	similar	enhanced	different

Passive-Active -
Tell me about the best job you ever had.

	Passive	Active
Answer:	People told me what to do	I just get things done
Motivation	Haven't you waited long enough	Just do it! Go for it!

Convincer strategy - How do you know if someone is good at their job? How many times do you need to (see, hear, read, do) to become convinced?

Answer:	see, hear, read, do
	once, number of times, over time, every time

If you find even better words or phrases to motivate each of these styles, email them to: lifestar@rmi.net or mail to: LifeStar, 2244 S. Olive St., Denver, CO 80224.

Bibliography

Barker, Joel, *Future Edge*, William Morrow, NY, 1992,

Charvet, Shelle Rose, *Words that Change Minds*, Kendall-Hunt, 1999.

Cialdini, Robert, *Influence–The Psychology of Persuasion*, William Morrow, NY, 1993.

Dilts, Robert, *Sleight of Mouth*, Meta Publications, Capitola, CA, (1999).

Faulkner, Charles, *The Mythic Wheel of Life*, Genesis II (audio), 1993.

Laborde, Genie, *Influencing with Integrity*, Syntony, Palo Alto, 1987.

Rogers, Everett, *The Diffusion of Innovations*, Free Press, 1995.

Schwartz, Peter, *Art of the Long View*, Doubleday, NY, 1996.